365
Inspirational Moments of Pope Francis

whitestar

On April 21, 2025, Pope Francis returned to the house of his Father, leaving behind a rich legacy of peace, tolerance, and compassion.

INTRODUCTION

Pope Francis's communication does not consist solely of words and it does not consist solely of gestures or even of contexts.

Instead, it is a sum of all these, to which one must add his immediacy of action and his ability to look around while firing questions, summarizing concepts and emphasizing the principal points of his discourse to such an extent that he delivers to a square filled with 50,000 listeners that which he would say to a class of 25 children.

Then there is his ability to transmit feelings through images drawn from his own experiences and those of people at large.

When, for the first time, Pope Francis greeted the square with "good morning" and concluded his speech with "enjoy your lunch," listeners immediately tuned in to him.

What is more down-to-earth than "enjoy your lunch" addressed to a throng of tourists on pilgrimages in Rome at 12:30 on a Sunday afternoon? Similarly, how firm is his language in the prayer for five fingers or to "the Madonna who unravels knots!"

There are also terms derived from the more immediate common language of social media, which he adopts as his own: from "God spray" to "babysitter Church." Likewise, his frequent references to novels and movies that he has read and seen; his gestures themselves consist of an original and up-to-date communicative mix.

Yet, even this is not enough to explain his great audience success. He transmits profound content through a series of keywords that are capable, in and of themselves, of ensuring the conversion of the individual and the community.

Below is a series of examples.

Let us begin with tenderness.

"We must not be afraid of goodness, not even of tenderness," in this way he started his speech in St. Peter's Square on March 19 2013, going on to say: "To take care

of something, to watch over it, requires goodness – requires that it be experienced with tenderness."

On April 7 2013, he reinterpreted the parable of the Prodigal Son: "Not for a single moment did the Father stop thinking about him with patience and love, with hope and mercy, and declaring – as he saw him from afar and ran out to meet and embrace him with tenderness, the tenderness of God, and without a single word of reproach – 'he has returned'."

Essentially, this word, like those that followed, was paradigmatic of his pastoral message as a whole.

Another word is mercy, when paired with the jubilee year. It must not only be applied to God, who by definition is mercy and the essence, the complete and utter Other, but must also become a manner of life and of approaching others.

Both the bishop, and every believer, must be merciful. Each and every person.

To enter into the logic of God is to enter into that of the very mercy of the Gospel and the Cross, which is not primarily that of pain and death, but rather that of love and the gift of self, which generates life.

"To follow," says Francis, "to accompany Christ, to stay at his side requires an 'exit,' a departure. A departure from oneself, from a tired and habitual manner of keeping faith, from the temptation to shut oneself out of one's own pattern of thought, which ends up shutting out God's future creative actions. God departed from himself in order to come into our midst, he pitched his tent among us in order to bring us his mercy, which brings salvation and offers hope. We too – if we wish to follow him and stay at his side – should not be content to linger in the compound of the ninety-nine sheep; we should 'exit,' search at his side for the lost sheep, the one farthest away."

Again, on September 10 2014, Pope Francis said: "The Church cannot repeat the same thing to her children: 'Like the Father and Jesus, be merciful'. Mercy. So, the Church behaves like Jesus. She does not give practical lessons on love or on mercy. She does not propagate a philosophy or a path of wisdom in the world... Certainly, Christianity is also all of this, a sheer consequence of reflection. Like Christ, the Mother Church teaches by example, and words illuminate the meaning of her gestures. The Church is a mother, teaching the works of mercy to her children."

Again, "Now is the time of mercy," he said forcefully in an airplane on July 28 2013. "The Church must go to minister to the wounded; it must find mercy for everyone... By not only by waiting for it, but by searching for it! That is mercy." Pope Francis seems to have adopted the view of Fyodor Dostoevsky – an author of whom he is well aware – in the "Brothers Karamazov," in which one reads: "All that is true and beautiful is always full of infinite mercy. Because, like the star in God's sky, mercy sparkles."

Another frequent word is mission.

"We often forget to be good Christians," he states, in a text that dates back to his years in Buenos Aires. "Thus begins the temptation to absolutize the spirituality of the spirituality of the layman, of the catechist, of the priest, with the serious danger of losing its origins and evangelical simplicity. And, once we lose the common reference point of the Christian, we run the risk of succumbing to snobbishness, of becoming easily influenced, of becoming like those who enjoy themselves and grow fat, who feed themselves but do not help others to grow. The parts become details, and by privileging those details we easily forget about the whole, about the fact that we are one and the same people. Then begin the centrifugal motions that have nothing of the missionary about them; if anything, they are the exact opposite. They scatter us, they destroy us, and, paradoxically, they leave us fettered

inside our close-mindedness. Let us not forget: the whole is greater than the part." Other words that return as a refrain include sin, corruption, testimony, hope, life, communion, humility, education, peace, faith, and people.

Speaking of sin and corruption, he says: "A corrupt heart – here lies sin. Why does a heart grow corrupt? The heart is not the last resort of a man closed in on himself; the relationship does not end there (not even the moral relationship). The human heart is a heart to the extent that it is capable of relating to another; to the extent that it is capable of love or of denying love (hate).

This is why Jesus, when he exhorts us to recognize the heart as the source of our actions, calls our attention to this ultimate acceptance of our restless heart: 'Wherever your treasure lies, there too will lie your heart' (Mt 6:21). Knowing a man's heart, its condition, necessarily entails knowing the treasure to which his heart refers, the treasure that liberates and fills, or destroys and reduces to slavery – in this last case, the treasure that corrupts. So that from the fact of corruption (personal or social) one passes to the heart as creator and preserver of this corruption, and from the heart one passes to the treasure to which this heart is attached."

Finding 365 thoughts for a year in the Magisterium of Pope Francis was easy but also difficult due to the profundity of his message, which is truly remarkable.

While submitting himself as a servo humilis before his interviewer and erasing all distance, Pope Francis offered messages from the depths of conscience, inviting us to austere asceticism but also toward a blue and safe sky. His words – as Cardinal Pietro Parolin has written – "open, embrace, and facilitate. They help lift our gaze outwards. They become seeds that are able to blossom in the most unexpected ways in the lives of those who listen to them: in a free and mysterious manner, like a gift of grace, beyond any pretence of 'function'."

1

Moreover, when our hearts are authentically open to universal communion, this sense of fraternity excludes nothing and no one.

2

How marvellous it would be if, at the end of the day, each of us could say: today I have performed an act of charity towards others!

3

The Christian is someone who can decrease so that the Lord may increase, in his heart and in the heart of others.

4

We have forgotten that we ourselves are dust of the earth; our very bodies are made up of her elements, we breathe her air and we receive life and refreshment from her waters.

5

The Child Jesus reveals the tenderness
of God's immense love surrounding
each one of us.

6

We need to rediscover a contemplative
spirit, so that the love of God
may warm our hearts.

7

Our common home is like a sister
with whom we share our life and
a beautiful mother who opens
her arms to embrace us.

8

The Creator does not abandon us;
he never forsakes his loving plan or repents
of having created us.

9

The climate is a common good, belonging to all and meant for all.
At the global level, it is a complex system linked to many
of the essential conditions for human life.

10

Fresh drinking water is an issue of primary importance, since it is indispensable for human life.

11

I cannot imagine a Christian
who does not know how to smile.
May we joyfully witness
to our faith.

12

Being a Christian is not just about
following commandments: it is about
letting Christ take possession of our lives
and transform them.

13

God does not reveal himself in strength or power,
but in the weakness and fragility of a newborn babe.

14

Accordingly, our human ability to transform
reality must proceed in line with God's
original gift of all that is.

15

Anyone who has grown up in the hills
or used to sit by the spring to drink,
or played outdoors in the neighbourhood
square; going back to these places is a chance
to recover something of their true selves.

16

All of us can cooperate as instruments
of God for the care of creation,
each according to his or her own culture,
experience, involvements and talents.

17

Every creature is thus the object of the Father's tenderness, who gives it its place in the world. Even the fleeting life of the least of beings is the object of his love, and in its few seconds of existence.

18

There can be no renewal of our relationship with nature
without a renewal of humanity itself.
There can be no ecology without an adequate anthropology.

19

Yet we are called to be instruments of God our Father,
so that our planet might be what he desired when he created it
and correspond with his plan for peace, beauty and fullness.

20

Each of us has his or her own personal identity and is capable of entering into dialogue with others and with God himself.

21

We can hardly consider ourselves to be fully loving if we disregard any aspect of reality.

22

Greater investment needs to be made in research aimed at understanding more fully the functioning of ecosystems and adequately analyzing the different variables associated with any significant modification of the environment.

23

Be committed to something, be committed to someone. This is the vocation of young people so don't be afraid to take a risk on the field, but play fairly and give it your best. Don't be afraid to give the best of yourselves! Don't look for easy solutions beforehand so as to avoid tiredness and struggle. And don't bribe the referee.

24

Today's media do enable us to communicate and to share our knowledge and affections. Yet at times they also shield us from direct contact with the pain, the fears and the joys of others and the complexity of their personal experiences.

25

The Church then, has the task of keeping
the lamp of hope burning and clearly visible,
so that it may continue to shine as a sure sign
of salvation and illuminate for all humanity
the path which leads to the encounter
with the merciful face of God.

26

A good educator focuses on the *essential*.
She doesn't get lost in details, but passes on what
really matters so the child or the student can
find the meaning and the joy of life. It's the truth.
In the Gospel the essential thing is *mercy*.

27

The elderly bring with them memory and the wisdom of experience, which warns us not to foolishly repeat our past mistakes. Young people call us to renewed and expansive hope, for they represent new directions for humanity and open us up to the future, lest we cling to a nostalgia for structures and customs which are no longer life-giving in today's world.

28

Let us learn to face moments of adversity with courage, certain that the Lord never fails to give his support and his grace to each of his children.

29

Like a grapevine, the people require great care, they require patient and devoted love. This is what God does with us, and this is what we Pastors are called to do.

30

The natural environment is a collective good, the patrimony of all humanity and the responsibility of everyone. If we make something our own, it is only to administer it for the good of all.

31

Nobody is suggesting a return to the Stone Age, but we do need to slow down and look at reality in a different way.

32

Ecological culture... Needs to be a distinctive way of looking at things, a way of thinking, policies, an educational programme, a lifestyle and a spirituality which together generate resistance to the assault of the technocratic paradigm.

33

The creation can only be understood as a gift from
the outstretched hand of the Father of all, and as a reality
illuminated by the love which calls us together
into universal communion.

34

When we fail to acknowledge as part of reality the worth
of a poor person, a human embryo, a person with disabilities –
to offer just a few examples – it becomes difficult to hear
the cry of nature itself.

35

Everything is related, and we human beings are united as brothers and sisters on a wonderful pilgrimage, woven together by the love God has for each of his creatures and which also unites us in fond affection with brother sun, sister moon, brother river and mother earth.

36

How wonderful is the certainty that each human life is not adrift in the midst of hopeless chaos, in a world ruled by pure chance or endlessly recurring cycles!

37

We cannot presume to heal our relationship with nature and the environment without healing all fundamental human relationships.

38

The created things of this world are
not free of ownership.

39

Human life is itself a gift which must be defended from various forms of debasement. Every effort to protect and improve our world entails profound changes in "lifestyles, models of production and consumption, and the established structures of power which today govern societies."

40

Interventions which affect the urban or rural landscape should take into account how various elements combine to form a whole which is perceived by its inhabitants as a coherent and meaningful framework for their lives.

41

Our relationship with the environment
can never be isolated from our relationship
with others and with God.

42

The violence present in our hearts, wounded
by sin, is also reflected in the symptoms of sickness
evident in the soil, in the water, in the air
and in all forms of life.

43

Challenges exist to be overcome!
Let us be realists, but without losing our joy,
our boldness and our hope-filled commitment.
Let us not allow ourselves to be robbed of missionary vigour!

44

[...] The analysis of environmental problems cannot be separated from the analysis of human, family, work-related and urban contexts, nor from how individuals relate to themselves, which leads in turn to how they relate to others and to the environment.

45

Let us read the Gospel, a small section each day. This way we will learn what is most essential in our lives: love and mercy.

46

When we do not adore God, we adore something else. Money and power are false idols which often take the place of God.

47

A wholesome social life can light up
a seemingly undesirable environment.

48

Some forms of pollution
are part of people's daily experience.

49

Environmental education should facilitate making the leap towards the transcendent which gives ecological ethics its deepest meaning.

50

To cite one example, most of the paper we produce is thrown away and not recycled.

51

Take care of God's creation.
But above all, take care of people in need.

52

[...] Yet all is not lost. Human beings, while capable of the worst, are also capable of rising above themselves, choosing again what is good, and making a new start, despite their mental and social conditioning.

53

We are always capable of going out of ourselves towards the other.

54

Such sobriety, when lived freely and consciously, is liberating. It is not a lesser life or one lived with less intensity. On the contrary, it is a way of living life to the full.

55

Happiness means knowing how to limit some needs which only diminish us, and being open to the many different possibilities which life can offer.

56

Worldwide there is minimal access to clean and renewable energy. There is still a need to develop adequate storage technologies.

57

A poor person who dies today of cold and hunger is not a news item, but if the stock markets of the major world capitals drop two or three points, it is a great global scandal.

58

Politics must pay greater attention to foreseeing new conflicts and addressing the causes which can lead to them.

59

We are not God. The earth was here before us and it has been given to us.

60

The Gospel speaks of a seed which, once sown, grows by itself, even as the farmer sleeps.

61

[....] God, who wishes to work with us
and who counts on our cooperation,
can also bring good out of the evil
we have done.

62

We are free to apply our intelligence
towards things evolving positively,
or towards adding new ills,
new causes of suffering
and real setbacks.

63

Each community can take from the bounty
of the earth whatever it needs for subsistence,
but it also has the duty to protect the earth and
to ensure its fruitfulness for coming generations.

64

A sense of deep communion with
the rest of nature cannot be real if our hearts
lack tenderness, compassion and concern
for our fellow human beings.

65

Good education plants seeds when we are young, and these continue to bear fruit throughout life.

66

True faith in the incarnate Son of God is inseparable from self-giving, from membership in the community, from service, from reconciliation with others.

67

The salvation which God offers us is the work of his mercy. No human efforts, however good they may be, can enable us to merit so great a gift. God, by his sheer grace, draws us to himself and makes us one with him.

68

Human ecology also implies another profound reality: the relationship between human life and the moral law, which is inscribed in our nature and is necessary for the creation of a more dignified environment.

69

Today, however, we have to realize that a true ecological approach *always* becomes a social approach; it must integrate questions of justice in debates on the environment, so as to hear *both the cry of the earth and the cry of the poor*.

70

It would hardly be helpful to describe symptoms without acknowledging the human origins of the ecological crisis.

71

No system can completely suppress
our openness to what is good,
true and beautiful, or our God-given
ability to respond to his grace
at work deep in our hearts.

72

An integral ecology is inseparable from
the notion of the common good,
a central and unifying principle
of social ethics.

73

Let us continue to wonder about the purpose and meaning of everything. Otherwise we would simply legitimate the present situation and need new forms of escapism to help us endure the emptiness.

74

Where we find hate and darkness, may we bring love and hope,
in order to give a more human face to society.

75

The parish is the presence of the Church
in a given territory, an environment for hearing God's word,
for growth in the Christian life, for dialogue, proclamation,
charitable outreach, worship and celebration.

76

When a society – whether local, national or global –
is willing to leave a part of itself on the fringes, no political
programmes or resources spent on law enforcement or
surveillance systems can indefinitely guarantee tranquility.

77

But until exclusion and inequality
in society and between peoples
are reversed, it will be impossible
to eliminate violence.

78

The individualism of our postmodern
and globalized era favours a lifestyle
which weakens the development
and stability of personal relationships
and distorts family bonds.

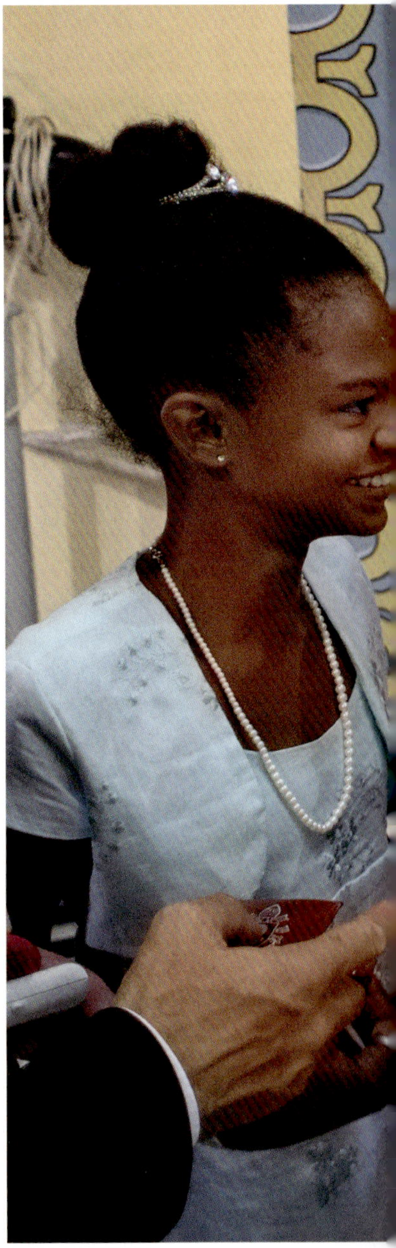

79

An integral ecology is also made up of simple daily gestures which break with the logic of violence, exploitation and selfishness. In the end, a world of exacerbated consumption is at the same time a world which mistreats life in all its forms.

80

What is called for is an evangelization capable of shedding light on these new ways of relating to God, to others and to the world around us, and inspiring essential values.

81

Human beings cannot be expected to feel responsibility for the world unless, at the same time, their unique capacities of knowledge, will, freedom and responsibility are recognized and valued.

82

Work is a necessity, part of the meaning of life on this earth, a path to growth, human development and personal fulfilment.

83

Recognizing the reasons why a given area is polluted requires a study of the workings of society, its economy, its behaviour patterns, and the ways it grasps reality.

84

Literal observance of the precepts is a fruitless exercise which does not change the heart and turn into practical behaviour: opening oneself to meet God and his Word in prayer, seeking justice and peace, taking care of the poor, the weak, the downtrodden.

85

With Jesus our life becomes full.
With him everything makes sense.

86

Nobody can go off to battle unless he is fully convinced of victory beforehand. If we start without confidence, we have already lost half the battle and we bury our talents.

87

To go out of ourselves and to join others is healthy for us. To be self-enclosed is to taste the bitter poison of immanence, and humanity will be worse for every selfish choice we make.

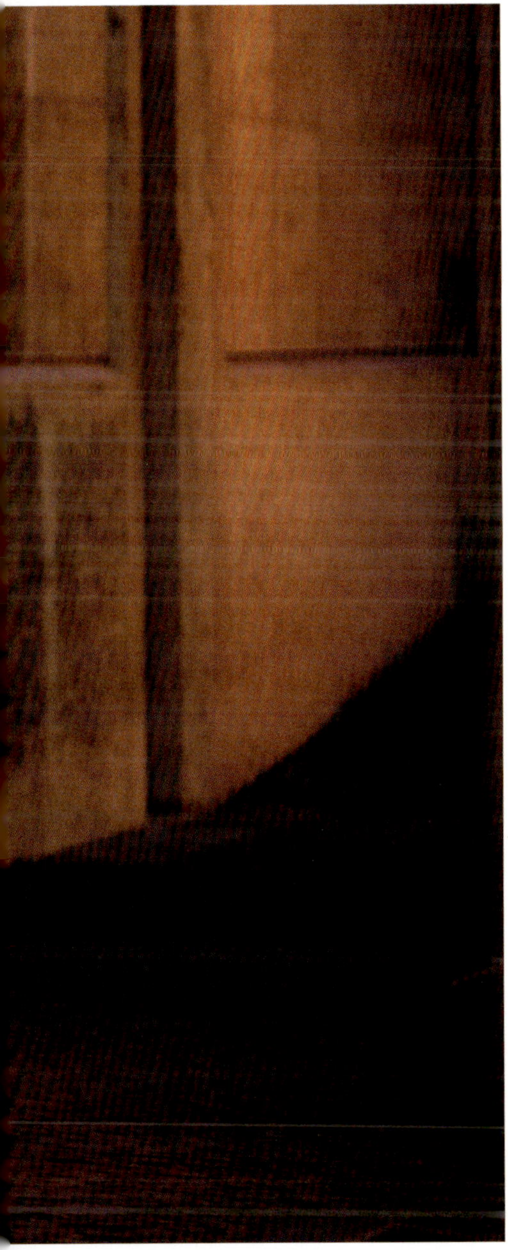

88

Many try to escape from others and take refuge in the comfort of their privacy or in a small circle of close friends, renouncing the realism of the social aspect of the Gospel.

89

Developing the created world in a prudent way is the best way of caring for it.

90

The gravity of the ecological crisis demands that we all look to the common good, embarking on a path of dialogue which demands patience, self-discipline and generosity, always keeping in mind that "realities are greater than ideas."

91

Death is an experience which touches all families, without exception. It is part of life; yet, where familial love is concerned, death never seems natural.

92

Hope is the virtue which goes places.
It isn't simply a path we take for the pleasure of it,
but it has an end, a goal which is practical and lights up our way.

93

Our loved ones are not lost in the darkness of nothing: hope assures us that they are in the good and strong hands of God. Love is stronger than death. Thus, the way is to let love grow, make it stronger, and love will guard us until the day that every tear shall be wiped away, when "death shall be no more, neither shall there be mourning nor crying nor pain any more."

94

Underlying the principle of the common good is respect for the human person as such, endowed with basic and inalienable rights ordered to his or her integral development.

95

The love of God is not generic. God looks with love upon every man and woman, calling them by name.

96

Meeting and welcoming within us Jesus, "Bread of Life", gives meaning and hope to the often winding journey of life.

97

The Church journeys among her people, in the history of men and women, of fathers and mothers, of sons and daughters: this is the history that matters to the Lord. The great events of worldly powers are written in history books, and there they will remain. But the history of human feelings is written directly in the heart of God; and that is the history that will endure for eternity. This is where life and faith are located.

98

We have had enough of immorality and the mockery of ethics, goodness, faith and honesty. It is time to acknowledge that light-hearted superficiality has done us no good.

99

We live in a society that leaves no room for God;
day by day this numbs our hearts.

100

Today more than ever we need men and women who, on the basis of their experience of accompanying others, are familiar with processes which call for prudence, understanding, patience and docility to the Spirit, so that they can protect the sheep from wolves who would scatter the flock.

101

Whenever a community receives the message of salvation, the Holy Spirit enriches its culture with the transforming power of the Gospel.

102

The social devaluation for the stable and generative alliance between man and woman is certainly a loss for everyone.

103

Love, overflowing with small gestures of mutual care, is also civic and political, and it makes itself felt in every action that seeks to build a better world.

104

Too often we participate in the globalization of indifference. May we strive instead to live global solidarity.

105

Spiritual worldliness, which hides behind the appearance of piety and even love for the Church, consists in seeking not the Lord's glory but human glory and personal well-being.

106

The faith cannot be constricted to the limits of understanding and expression of any one culture. It is an indisputable fact that no single culture can exhaust the mystery of our redemption in Christ.

107

It is more difficult to allow God
to encounter us than to encounter God,
because we always resist.

108

Sometimes we cast the elderly aside, but they are a precious treasure: to cast them aside is an injustice and an irreparable loss.

109

Remembering the dead, caring for their graves and prayers of suffrage, are the testimony of confident hope, rooted in the certainty that death does not have the last word on human existence, for man is destined to a life without limits, which has its roots and its fulfillment in God.

110

We must be a gift for others and allow the Holy Spirit to turn us into instruments of acceptance, instruments of reconciliation, instruments of forgiveness.

111

Sanctity is understood, then, not as a prerogative of the few: sanctity is a gift offered to all, no one excluded, by which the distinctive character of every Christian is constituted.

112

We are not asked to be flawless, but to keep growing and wanting to grow as we advance along the path of the Gospel; our arms must never grow slack.

113

Jesus Christ has a universal destination.
Its mandate of charity encompasses all dimensions of existence, all individuals, all areas of community life, and all peoples.
Nothing human can be alien to it.

114

Let us renew our confidence in preaching,
based on the conviction that it is God
who seeks to reach out to others through the preacher,
and that he displays his power through human words.

115

But if we allow doubts and fears to dampen our courage, instead of being creative we will remain comfortable and make no progress whatsoever. In this case we will not take an active part in historical processes, but become mere onlookers as the Church gradually stagnates.

116

In itself mercy is the greatest of the virtues, since all the others revolve around it and, more than this, it makes up for their deficiencies.

CLEMENS·X·PONT·MAX·
ANNO·IVBILEI·MDCLXXV·

117

The homily is the touchstone for judging a pastor's closeness and ability to communicate to his people.

118

The joy of the Gospel fills the hearts and lives of all who encounter Jesus.

119

Preparation for preaching is so important a task that a prolonged time of study, prayer, reflection and pastoral creativity should be devoted to it.

120

Rather, there is a need to incorporate the history, culture and architecture of each place, thus preserving its original identity.

121

We incarnate the duty of hearing
the cry of the poor when we are deeply
moved by the suffering of others.

122

Sometimes we prove hard of heart and mind;
we are forgetful, distracted and carried away by
the limitless possibilities for consumption and
distraction offered by contemporary society.

123

The great danger in today's world, pervaded as it is by consumerism, is the desolation and anguish born of a complacent yet covetous heart, the feverish pursuit of frivolous pleasures, and a blunted conscience.

124

Going out to others in order to reach the fringes of humanity does not mean rushing out aimlessly into the world. Often it is better simply to slow down, to put aside our eagerness in order to see and listen to others, to stop rushing from one thing to another and to remain with someone who has faltered along the way.

125

To sustain a lifestyle which excludes others, or to sustain enthusiasm for that selfish ideal, a globalization of indifference has developed. Almost without being aware of it, we end up being incapable of feeling compassion at the outcry of the poor, and, weeping for other people's pain.

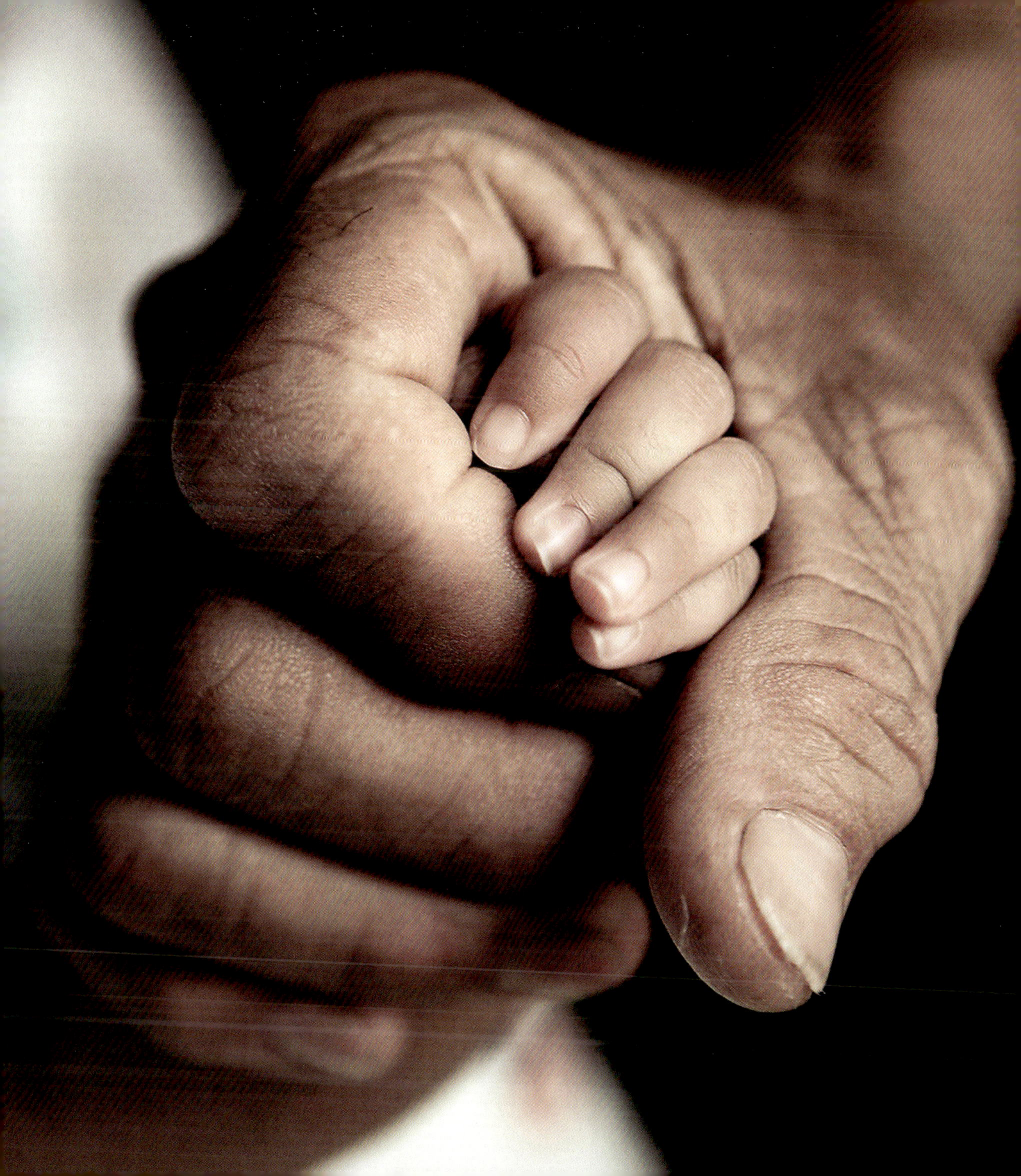

126

Wherever there is life, fervour and a desire to bring Christ to others, genuine vocations will arise.

127

Each meaningful economic decision made in one part of the world has repercussions everywhere else; consequently, no government can act without regard for shared responsibility.

128

Seeking happiness in material things
is a sure way of being unhappy.

129

Believing in Jesus means making him the centre, the meaning of our life. Christ is not an optional element: he is the "Living Bread", the essential nourishment. Binding oneself to him, in a true relationship of faith and love, does not mean being tied down, but being profoundly free, always on the journey.

130

What is needed is the ability to cultivate
an interior space which can give a Christian meaning
to commitment and activity.

131

Whenever our eyes are opened to acknowledge
the other, we grow in the light of faith
and knowledge of God.

132

To care for children, and to help young people to embrace noble ideals,
is a guarantee of the future of society.

133

With a tenderness which never disappoints,
but is always capable of restoring our joy,
he makes it possible for us to lift up our heads and to start anew.

134

I invite everyone to be bold and creative in this task
of rethinking the goals, structures, style and methods
of evangelization in their respective communities.

135

At this time of crisis it is important not to become closed in on oneself, but rather to be open and attentive towards others.

136

Welcome and care, closeness and attention, trust and hope, are likewise basic promises, which can be summed up in a single word: love.

137

There also exists a constant tension between ideas and realities. Realities simply are, whereas ideas are worked out. There has to be continuous dialogue between the two, lest ideas become detached from realities.

138

Faith is not fearful of reason; on the contrary, it seeks and trusts reason, since “the light of reason and the light of faith both come from God” and cannot contradict each other.

139

A supposed soundness of doctrine or discipline leads instead to a narcissistic and authoritarian elitism, whereby instead of evangelizing, one analyzes and classifies others, and instead of opening the door to grace, one exhausts his or her energies in inspecting and verifying. In neither case is one really concerned about Jesus Christ or others.

140

The human heart desires joy.
We all desire joy, every family,
every people aspires to happiness.

141

The spirit of love which reigns in a family guides
both mother and child in their conversations;
therein they teach and learn, experience correction
and grow in appreciation of what is good.
Something similar happens in a homily.

142

But the Church is not a tollhouse;
it is the house of the Father, where there is
a place for everyone, with all their problems.

143

Faith always remains something of a cross;
it retains a certain obscurity which does not
detract from the firmness of its assent.

144

True charity requires courage: let us overcome the fear
of getting our hands dirty so as to help those in need.

145

Christ the pastor is a careful guide who participates in the life of his flock,
does not seek other interests, has no ambition other than guiding,
feeding and protecting his sheep.

146

My words are not those of a foe or an opponent. I am interested only in helping those who are in thrall to an individualistic, indifferent and self-centred mentality to be freed from those unworthy chains and to attain a way of living and thinking which is more humane, noble and fruitful, and which will bring dignity to their presence on this earth.

147

There is so much noise in the world! May we learn to be silent in our hearts and before God.

148

Each culture and social group needs purification and growth.

149

We must have sincere trust in our fellow pilgrims, putting aside all suspicion or mistrust, and turn our gaze to what we are all seeking: the radiant peace of God's face. Trusting others is an art and peace is an art.

150

Life is a precious gift, but we realize this only when we give it to others.

151

The family is the first school for the young, the best home for the elderly. The family constitutes the best "social capital." It cannot be replaced by other institutions. It needs to be helped and strengthened, lest we lose our proper sense of the services which society as a whole provides.

152

Christ's resurrection is not an event of the past; it contains a vital power which has permeated this world. Where all seems to be dead, signs of the resurrection suddenly spring up. It is an irresistible force.

153

Intimacy with God, in itself incomprehensible, is revealed by images which speak to us of communion, communication, self-giving and love.

154

There is a relationship between our life and that of mother earth, between the way we live and the gift we have received from God.

155

If politics is dominated by financial speculation, or if the economy is ruled solely by a technocratic and utilitarian paradigm concerned with maximum production, we will not grasp, much less resolve, the great problems of humanity.

156

Each of us is just one part of a complex and differentiated whole, interacting in time: peoples who struggle to find meaning, a destiny, and to live with dignity, to "live well", and in that sense, worthily.

REDIPUGLIA 2014
03

157

We are brothers and sisters because God created us out of love and destined us, purely of his own initiative, to be his sons and daughters.

158

And how beautiful it would be if all could admire how much we care for one another, how we encourage and help each other.

159

The Church which "goes forth" is a community
of missionary disciples who take the first step,
who are involved and supportive,
who bear fruit and rejoice.

160

The Pope loves everyone, rich and poor alike,
but he is obliged in the name of Christ
to remind all that the rich must help,
respect and promote the poor.

SEPTVAGIES SEPTIES

161

God did not will creation for himself,
so he could see himself reflected in it.
On the contrary: creation is a gift to be shared.

162

The mission is a constant stimulus
not to remain mired in mediocrity
but to continue growing.

163

God always desires to build bridges;
we are the ones who build walls!
And those walls always fall down!

164

Let us keep a place for Christ in our lives,
let us care for one another and let us
be loving custodians of creation.

165

Personal initiatives are always necessary and good. But we are asked to go one step further: to start viewing reality in an organic and not fragmented way, to ask about where we stand in relation to others, inasmuch as "everything is interconnected." There is no right to exclusion.

166

The Eucharist joins heaven and earth; it embraces and penetrates all creation. The world which came forth from God's hands returns to him in blessed and undivided adoration: in the bread of the Eucharist, "creation is projected towards divinization, towards the holy wedding feast, towards unification with the Creator himself."

167

God loves us. We must not be afraid to love him. The faith is professed with the lips and with the heart, through words and through love.

168

We can no longer trust in the unseen forces and the invisible hand of the market. Growth in justice requires more than economic growth, while presupposing such growth: it requires decisions, programmes, mechanisms and processes specifically geared to a better distribution of income, the creation of sources of employment and an integral promotion of the poor which goes beyond a simple welfare mentality.

169

Jesus never detracts from the dignity of anyone, no matter how little they possess or seem capable of contributing. He takes everything as it comes.

170

Corruption is a greater ill than sin.
More than forgiveness,
this ill must be treated.

171

It must be acknowledged that none of the grave problems of humanity can be resolved without interaction between states and peoples at the international level. Every significant action carried out in one part of the planet has universal, ecological, social and cultural repercussions.

172

Our society benefits when each person and social group feels truly at home. In a family, parents, grandparents and children feel at home; no one is excluded. If someone has a problem, even a serious one, even if he brought it upon himself, the rest of the family comes to his assistance; they support him.

173

The unified and complete sense of human life that the Gospel proposes is the best remedy for the ills of our cities.

174

There are Christians whose lives seem like Lent without Easter.

175

History is made by each generation as it follows
in the footsteps of those preceding it,
as it seeks its own path and respects
the values which God has placed
in the human heart.

176

The corrupt one does not perceive
his corruption. It is somewhat like what happens
with bad breath: the person who has it is seldom
aware of it; it is the others who notice it
and have to tell him about it.

177

I don't have much more to give you or to offer you, but
I want to share with you what I do have and what I love.
It is Jesus Christ, the mercy of the Father.

178

Beware of the temptation of jealousy! We are all in the same
boat and headed to the same port! Let us ask for the grace to rejoice
in the gifts of each, which belong to all.

179

Faith brings us closer. It makes us neighbors.
It makes us neighbors to others.
Faith awakens our commitment to others,
faith awakens our solidarity.

180

There is a bitter root which causes damage,
great damage, and silently destroys so many lives.
There is an evil which, bit by bit,
finds a place in our hearts and eats away
at our life: it is isolation.

181

God never closes off horizons; he is never unconcerned about the lives and sufferings of his children. God never allows himself to be outdone in generosity.

182

Freedom is a gift that God gives us, but we have to know how to accept it. We have to be able to have a free heart, because we all know that in the world there are so many things that bind our hearts and prevent them from being free.

183

[...] The Lord does not give the same things to everyone in the same way: He knows us personally and entrusts us with what is right for us; but in everyone, in all, there is something equal: the same, immense trust. God trusts us, God has hope in us! And this is the same for everyone. Let us not disappoint Him! Let us not be misled by fear, but let us reciprocate trust with trust!

184

War is the negation of all rights and a dramatic assault on the environment. If we want true integral human development for all, we must work tirelessly to avoid war between nations and peoples.

185

Serving means caring for their vulnerability. Caring for the vulnerable of our families, our society, our people.

186

It is our duty to know how to administer our goods, for they are a gift from God. But when these goods enter your heart and begin to take over your life, that's where you can get lost.

187

In the daily reality of life, there has to be room for dreaming. A young person incapable of dreaming is cut off, self-enclosed.

188

A path of hope calls for a culture of encounter, dialogue, which can overcome conflict and sterile confrontation.

189

Optimism is a state of mind. Tomorrow, you wake up in a bad mood and you're not optimistic at all; you see everything in a bad light. Hope is something more. Hope involves suffering. Hope can accept suffering as part of building something; it is able to sacrifice.

190

Our faith makes us leave our homes and go forth to encounter others, to share their joys, their hopes and their frustrations. Our faith, "calls us out of our house", to visit the sick, the prisoner and to those who mourn. It makes us able to laugh with those who laugh, and rejoice with our neighbors who rejoice.

191

The spirit of prayer gives time back to God, it steps away from the obsession of a life that is always lacking time, it rediscovers the peace of necessary things, and discovers the joy of unexpected gifts.

192

Even if we have made mistakes in our life, the Lord never tires of showing us the path to return to and to encounter Him. Jesus' love for each of us is the source of consolation and hope.

193

Do not be afraid of solidarity, service and offering a helping hand, so that no one is excluded from the path.

194

Fraternal charity, the living expression of the new commandment of Jesus, is expressed in programs, works and institutions which work for the integral development of the person, as well as for the care and protection of those who are most vulnerable.

195

All of us make mistakes in life and all of us, too, are sinners.
And when we go to ask the Lord for forgiveness for our sins, for our mistakes,
He always forgives us, He never tires of forgiving.

196

Laying down one's life out of love is not easy.
As with the Master, "staking everything"
can sometimes involve the cross.
Times when everything seems uphill.

197

Even if it is not always easy to approach young people, progress has been made in two areas: the awareness that the entire community is called to evangelize and educate the young, and the urgent need for the young to exercise greater leadership.

198

Kindness and the ability to say "thank you" are often considered a sign of weakness and raise the suspicion of others. This tendency is encountered even within the nucleus of the family. We must become firmly determined to educate others to be grateful and appreciative: the dignity of the person and social justice must both pass through the portal of the family.

199

I want to be a witness of the joy of the Gospel and bring
to you the tenderness and caress of God, our Father,
especially to his children most in need, to the elderly,
the sick, the imprisoned, the poor, to those who are victims
of this throw-away culture.

200

Jesus keeps knocking on our doors, the doors of our lives.
He doesn't do this by magic, with special effects, with flashing lights
and fireworks. Jesus keeps knocking on our door
in the faces of our brothers and sisters, in the faces of our neighbors,
in the faces of those at our side.

201

Ecology is essential for the survival of mankind; it is a moral issue which affects all of us.

202

Our God is a patient father, who always waits for us and waits with his heart in hand to welcome us, to forgive us. He always forgives us if we go to him.

203

In effect, ethics leads to a God who calls
for a committed response which is outside
the categories of the marketplace.

204

To read a passage of the Gospel every day; and to carry a little Gospel with us,
in our pocket, in a purse, in some way, to keep it at hand.
And there, reading a passage, we will find Jesus.

205

Ethics would make it possible to bring about balance and a more humane social order.

206

The evil spirit of defeatism is brother to the temptation to separate, before its time, the wheat from the weeds; it is the fruit of an anxious and self-centred lack of trust.

207

Do not forget: Gospel, Eucharist, Prayer. Thanks to these gifts of the Lord we are able to conform not to the world but to Christ, and follow him on his path, the path of "losing one's life."

208

To reprove a brother is a service, and it is possible and effective only if each one recognizes oneself to be a as sinner and in need of the Lord's forgiveness. The same awareness that enables me to recognize the fault of another.

209

It is important to know this. The rule of hospitality has always been sacred in the simplest Christian families: there is always a plate and a bed for the one in need.

210

We have to remember that the majority of our contemporaries are barely living from day to day, with dire consequences.

211

When adults lose their head, when each one thinks only of him- or herself, when a dad and mom hurt one another, the souls of their children suffer terribly, they experience a sense of despair. And these wounds leave a mark that lasts their whole lives.

212

God gives this quality, this charism to this person, not for himself, but in order that he may put it at the service of the whole community.

213

Some resist giving themselves over completely to mission and thus end up in a state of paralysis and acedia.

214

Do not lower our gaze, concerned only with our concerns,
but raise it constantly toward the horizons which God
opens before us and which surpass all that
we ourselves can foresee or plan.

215

A Christian must necessarily be merciful,
because this is the centre of the Gospel.
And faithful to this teaching, the Church
can only repeat the same thing to her children:
"Be merciful", as the Father is, and as Jesus was. Mercy.

216

Do not stand still. We all have to walk, to take a step every day, with the Lord's help. God is Father, he is mercy, he always loves us. If we seek Him, He welcomes us and forgives us.

217

It's not enough to love those who love us. Jesus says that pagans do this. It's not enough to do good to those who do good to us. To change the world for the better it is necessary to do good to those who are not able to return the favour, as the Father has done with us, by giving us Jesus.

218

Dear friends, let us therefore proceed toward full unity! History has separated us, but we are on the path toward reconciliation and communion! And this is true! And we must defend it! We are all on the path toward communion.

219

The goodness of God has no bounds
and does not discriminate against anyone.
For this reason the banquet of the Lord's gifts
is universal, for everyone.

220

Solidarity is a spontaneous reaction
by those who recognize that the social function
of property and the universal destination
of goods are realities which come before
private property.

francesco
caritas

221

You see, Christian hope is not simply a desire, a wish, it is not optimism: for a Christian, hope is expectation, fervent expectation, impassioned by the ultimate and definitive fulfilment of a mystery, the mystery of God's love, in which we are born again and which are already experiencing.

222

The Christian seed at the root of equality between spouses must bear new fruit today. The witness of the social dignity of marriage shall become persuasive precisely in this way, the way of a testimony which attracts, the way of reciprocity between them, of complementarity between them.

223

The heart that knows how to say 'thank you' is a good heart, it is a noble heart, it is a heart that is content.

224

You cannot love God without loving your neighbour and you cannot love your neighbour without loving God.

225

Our faith is challenged to discern how wine can come from water and how wheat can grow in the midst of weeds.

226

Popular piety enables us to see how the faith, once received, becomes embodied in a culture and is constantly passed on.

227

"Giving of oneself" means letting all the power of that love which is God's Holy Spirit take root in our lives, opening our hearts to his creative power. And giving of oneself even in the most difficult moments.

228

As usual, Jesus sets before us the "logic" of love. A mindset, an approach to life, which is capable of being lived out by all, because it is meant for all.

229

The flowing water is also a symbol of our tears.
Tears at so much devastation and ruin,
past and present.

230

Peace is not simply the absence of war, but a general condition
in which the human person is in harmony with him/herself,
in harmony with nature and in harmony with others.
This is peace.

231

When Jesus becomes part of our lives, we can no longer remain imprisoned by our past. Instead, we begin to look to the present, and we see it differently, with a different kind of hope.

232

Having faith does not mean having no difficulties, but having the strength to face them, knowing we are not alone.

233

Jesus is not a figure from the past: he continues now and always to light the way for us.

234

Sanctity is a gift, it is a gift granted to us by the Lord Jesus, when He takes us to Himself and clothes us in Himself, He makes us like Him.

235

Just as goodness tends to spread, the toleration of evil, which is injustice, tends to expand its baneful influence and quietly to undermine any political and social system, no matter how solid it may appear.

236

We need to care for the earth so that it may continue, as God willed, to be a source of life for the entire human family.

237

Faith is a light which does not blind; ideologies blind, the faith does not blind; it is a light which does not confuse, but which illuminates and respectfully guides the consciences and history of every person and society.

238

Without family, without the warmth of home, life grows empty, there is a weakening of the networks which sustain us in adversity, the networks which nurture us in daily living and motivate us to build a better future.

239

We need to grow in a solidarity which "would allow all peoples to become the artisans of their destiny", since "every person is called to self-fulfilment."

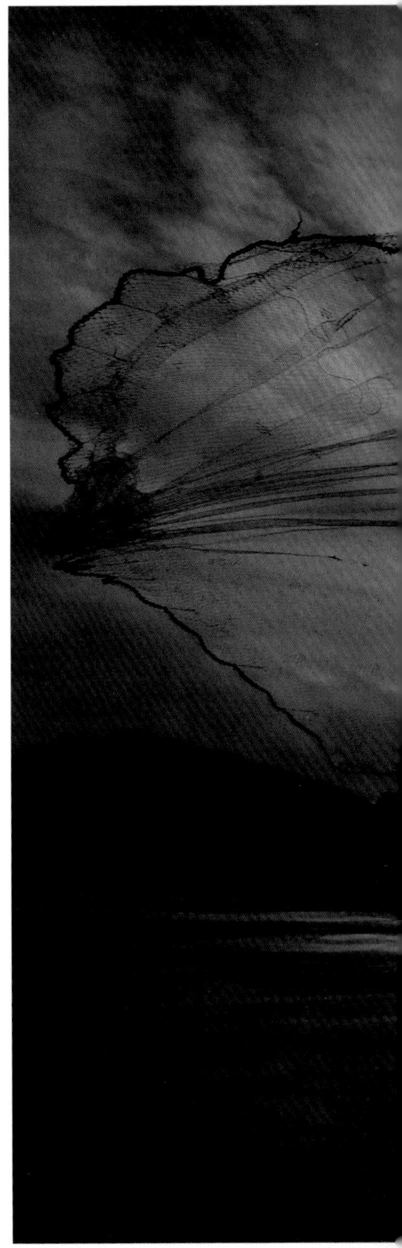

240

A joy already real and tangible now,
because *Jesus himself is our joy*,
and with Jesus joy finds its home.

241

We are all called to combat every form of slavery and to build fraternity – all of us, each one according to his or her own responsibility.

242

To have faith does not mean to never have difficult moments but to have the strength to face those moments knowing that we are not alone. And this is the peace that God gives to his children.

243

The homily cannot be a form of entertainment like those presented by the media, yet it does need to give life and meaning to the celebration.

244

We cannot follow Jesus on the path of love unless we first love others, unless we force ourselves to work together, to understand each other and to forgive each another, recognizing our own limits and mistakes. We must do works of mercy and with mercy! Putting our heart in them. Works of charity with love, with tenderness and always with humility!

245

Regarding this love, regarding this mercy, the divine grace poured into our hearts, one single thing is asked in return: *unreserved giving*. Not one of us can buy salvation!

246

Prayer is the soul's breath: it is important to find moments throughout the day to open your heart to God, even with simple and brief prayers of the Christian people.

247

Everything is a gift out of his love for us.

248

The homily can actually be an intense and happy experience of the Spirit, a consoling encounter with God's word, a constant source of renewal and growth.

249

Peace in society cannot be understood as pacification or the mere absence of violence resulting from the domination of one part of society over others.

250

The dignity of the human person and the common good rank higher than the comfort of those who refuse to renounce their privileges.

251

Jesus is He who brings generations closer.
He is the font of that love which unites families and people,
conquering all diffidence, all isolation, all distance.

252

In our world, especially in some countries, different forms of war and conflict are re-emerging, yet we Christians remain steadfast in our intention to respect others, to heal wounds, to build bridges, to strengthen relationships and to "bear one another's burdens."

253

A good relationship between the young
and the elderly is crucial for the journey
of the civil and ecclesial community.

254

The culture of prosperity deadens us;
we are thrilled if the market offers
us something new to purchase.
In the meantime all those lives
stunted for lack of opportunity seem
a mere spectacle; they fail to move us.

255

But our life is also thinking, reasoning. And this is important because we are animals who think; we don't think like animals! We are animals who think. Thinking, the language of the mind, is important.

POLICE

256

The heart of man may reject the light
and prefer the shadows, because light
lays bare his evil deeds.
Those who do evil hate light.
Those who do evil hate peace.

257

This contrast causes painful suffering. In many parts of the world, cities are the scene of mass protests where thousands of people call for freedom, a voice in public life, justice and a variety of other demands which, if not properly understood, will not be silenced by force.

258

But we need to create still broader opportunities for a more incisive female presence in the Church. Because "the feminine genius is needed in all expressions in the life of society, the presence of women must also be guaranteed in the workplace."

259

At a time when we most need a missionary dynamism which will bring salt and light to the world, many lay people fear that they may be asked to undertake some apostolic work and they seek to avoid any responsibility that may take away from their free time.

260

We need to pay attention to the global so as to avoid narrowness and banality. Yet we also need to look to the local, which keeps our feet on the ground.

261

The dignity of each human person and the pursuit of the common good are concerns which ought to shape all economic policies. At times, however, they seem to be a mere addendum imported from without in order to fill out a political discourse lacking in perspectives or plans for true and integral development.

262

In the effort to overcome a spirit of constant conflict, unity is always better than conflict.

263

Let us say NO to an economy of exclusion and inequality, where money rules, rather than service. That economy kills.

264

In a culture paradoxically suffering from anonymity and
at the same time obsessed with the details of other people's lives,
shamelessly given over to morbid curiosity,
the Church must look more closely and sympathetically
at others whenever necessary.

265

A life of remembrance needs others.
It demands exchange, encounter and a genuine solidarity capable of entering into the mindset of taking, blessing and giving.
It demands the logic of love.

266

It is good to grasp the kind of continuity and deep communion there is between the Church in Heaven and that which is still a pilgrim on earth. Those who already live in the sight of God can indeed sustain us and intercede for us, pray for us.

267

We must convince ourselves, despite every appearance to the contrary, that harmony is always possible, on every level and in every situation. There is no future without proposals and plans for peace! There is no future without peace!

268

One of the faults which we occasionally observe in sociopolitical activity is that spaces and power are preferred to time and processes. Giving priority to space means madly attempting to keep everything together in the present, trying to possess all the spaces of power and of self-assertion; it is to crystallize processes and presume to hold them back.

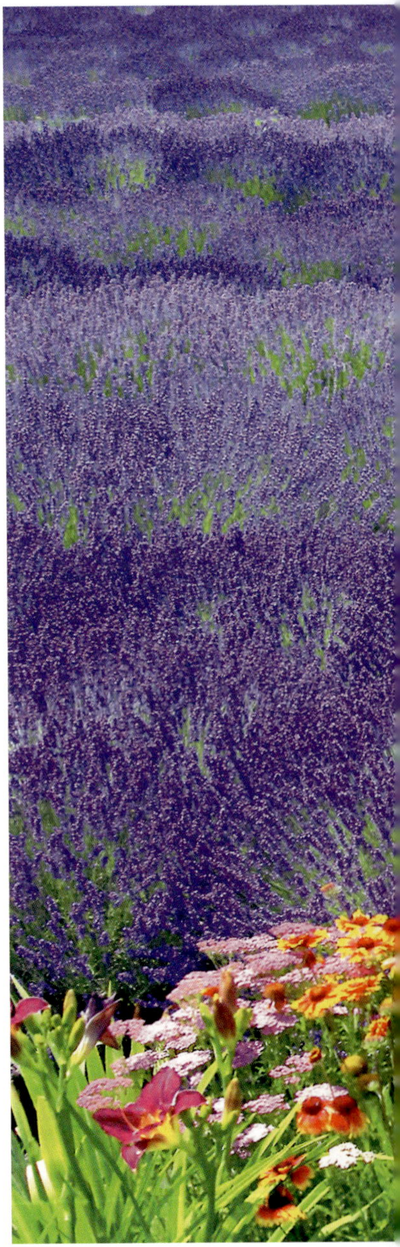

269

We have to be careful to avoid judgmental looks
and renew our belief in the transforming look
to which Jesus invites us.

270

Hope is the virtue which goes places.
It isn't simply a path we take for the pleasure of it,
but it has an end, a goal which is practical
and lights up our way.

271

The Church, community of mankind sanctified by the Blood of Christ and by Spirit of the Risen Lord, asks each one of us to be consistent with the gift of the faith and to undertake a journey of Christian witness.

272

We can no longer divide prayer,
the encounter with God in the Sacraments,
from listening to the other, closeness to his life,
especially to his wounds. Remember this:
love is the measure of faith.

273

Our witness is to make others understand
what it means to be Christian.

274

God is certainly truth, God is certainly good,
God certainly knows how to make things, he created the world.
But above all, God is beautiful!

275

It's up to us to become good soil with neither thorns nor stones, but tilled and cultivated with care, so it may bear good fruit for us and for our brothers and sisters.

276

New cultures are constantly being born in these vast new expanses where Christians are no longer the customary interpreters or generators of meaning. Instead, they themselves take from these cultures new languages, symbols, messages and paradigms which propose new approaches to life, approaches often in contrast with the Gospel of Jesus.

277

Better yet, it means learning to find Jesus in the faces of others, in their voices, in their pleas. And learning to suffer in the embrace of the crucified Jesus whenever we are unjustly attacked or meet with ingratitude, never tiring of our decision to live in fraternity.

278

Jesus' whole life, his way of dealing with the poor, his actions, his integrity, his simple daily acts of generosity, and finally his complete self-giving, is precious and reveals the mystery of his divine life.

279

We are in an age of knowledge and information, which has led to new and often anonymous kinds of power.

280

Evangelizing entails attracting by our witness those who are far off, it means humbly drawing near to those who feel distant from God in the Church, drawing near to those who feel judged and condemned outright by those who consider themselves to be perfect and pure.

281

If a text was written to console, it should not be used to correct errors; if it was written as an exhortation, it should not be employed to teach doctrine.

282

That is why we are called to always nourish great faith and hope for every person and his or her salvation: even those who seem far from the Lord are followed – or better yet "chased" – by his passionate love, by his faithful and also humble love.

283

The mother, despite being highly lauded from a symbolic point of view – many poems, many beautiful things said poetically of her – is rarely listened to or helped in daily life, rarely considered central to society in her role.

284

The Commandment to love God and neighbour is the first,
not because it is at the top of the list of Commandments.
Jesus does not place it at the pinnacle but at the centre,
because it is from the heart that everything must go out and
to which everything must return and refer.

285

Young people often fail to find responses to their concerns,
needs, problems and hurts in the usual structures.
As adults, we find it hard to listen patiently to them,
to appreciate their concerns and demands, and to speak
to them in a language they can understand.

286

Our unity can hardly shine forth if spiritual worldliness makes us feud among ourselves in a futile quest for power, prestige, pleasure or economic security.

287

There is no doubt that we must do far more to advance women, if we want to give more strength to the reciprocity between man and woman.

288

We must open ourselves to the peripheries, also acknowledging that, at the margins too, even one who is cast aside and scorned by society is the object of God's generosity.

289

Entering into the life of another, even when that person already has a part to play in our life, demands the sensitivity of a non-invasive attitude which renews trust and respect.

290

Men speak much of light, but they often
prefer the deceptive tranquillity of darkness.
We speak a lot about peace,
but we often turn to war or choose
the complicity of silence, or do nothing
concrete to build peace.

291

The People of God are called
to contemplate this light. A light for the
nations, as the elderly Simeon joyfully
expressed it. A light meant to shine on every
corner of this city, on our fellow citizens,
on every part of our lives.

292

Do not add to the troubles of an angry mind,
nor delay your gift to a beggar. Do not reject an afflicted suppliant,
nor turn your face away from the poor.

293

Within the realm of family bonds, the illness of our loved ones
is endured with an "excess" of suffering and anguish.
It is love that makes us feel this "excess."

294

The Church, at the beginning of her life and of her mission in the world, was but a community constituted to confess faith in Jesus Christ the Son of God and Redeemer of Man, a faith which operates through love.

295

A new civil ethic will arrive only when the leaders of public life reorganize the social bond beginning with the perverse struggle that spirals between the family and poverty, which leads us into the abyss.

296

Even the best families need support, and it takes a lot of patience to support one another! But such is life. Life is not lived in a laboratory, but in reality. Jesus himself experienced a family upbringing.

297

Don't let yourselves be robbed of hope and keep going! May they not steal it from you! On the contrary: spread hope!

298

The scandalous concentration of global wealth is made possible by the connivance of public leaders with the powers that be. Corruption is in and of itself a death process: when a life is ended, there is corruption.

299

Let's look at Jesus: he is our joy but also our strength, our certainty because he is the sure path: humility, solidarity, service. There is no other way.

300

My position, my ideas and my plans will move forward if I can prevail over others and impose my will and discard them. In this way we build up a culture of waste which today has reached worldwide proportions.

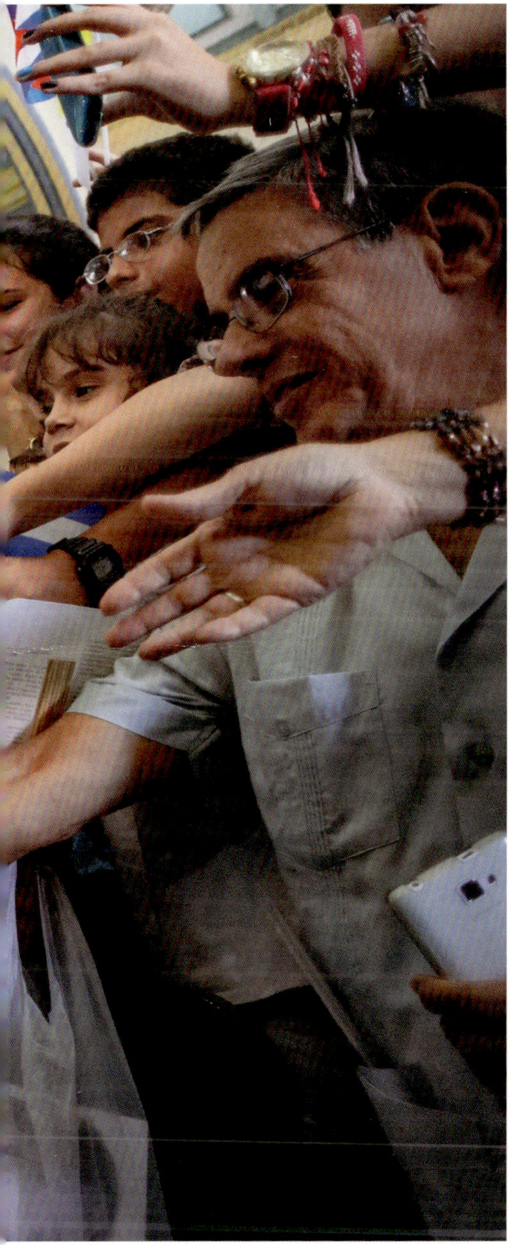

301

We must not forget, however,
that the Church is not only the priests,
or we bishops, no, she is all of us!
The Church is all of us! Agreed?

302

Our words can do much good
and also much harm; they can heal and
they can wound; they can encourage
and they can dishearten.

303

Mission is never the fruit of a perfectly planned program or a well-organized manual. Mission is always the fruit of a life which knows what it is to be found and healed, encountered and forgiven. Mission is born of a constant experience of God's merciful anointing.

304

Love is free. Charity, love is life choice, it is a way of being, a way of life, it is a path of humility and of solidarity. There is no other way for this love: to be humble and in solidarity with others.

305

Evangelization does not consist
in proselytizing.

306

Christ's humility is not moralism or a feeling.
Christ's humility is real; it is the choice
of being small, of staying with the lowliest
and with the marginalized, staying among
all of us sinners.

307

And a jealous heart is a sour heart, a heart
which seems to have vinegar instead of blood;
it is a heart that is never happy, it is a heart
which dismembers the community.

308

War does not begin on the battlefield:
war, wars begin in the heart,
with misunderstanding, division,
envy, with this struggle with others.

309

Therefore following Jesus on the path of charity, going with him to the existential outskirts.

310

Christ is the model for the Church, because the Church is his body. He is the model for all Christians, for us all. When one looks to Christ, one does not err.

311

Today there is need for people to be witnesses
to the mercy and tenderness of God, who spurs the resigned,
enlivens the disheartened, ignites the fire of hope.

312

We are all called to comfort our brothers and sisters, to testify that God alone can eliminate the causes of existential and spiritual tragedies.

313

The most important thing is what God does for us: he takes us by the hand and helps us to go forward. And this is called hope!

314

Every child who is marginalized, abandoned, who lives on the street begging with every kind of trick, without schooling, without medical care, is a cry that rises up to God and denounces the system that we adults have set in place.

315

The Child Jesus. My thoughts turn to all those children today who are killed and ill-treated, be they infants killed in the womb, deprived of that generous love of their parents and then buried in the egoism of a culture that does not love life.

316

How many people feel superior to others! We, too, often say as did that Pharisee in the parable: "I thank you, Lord, that I am not like that one, I am superior."

317

And do not forget: Christian consistency, which is to think, feel and live as a Christian, and not to think like a Christian and live as a pagan: not this!

318

Giving one's life does not only mean being killed; giving one's life, having the spirit of a martyr, it is in giving in duty, in silence, in prayer, in honest fulfilment of his duty; in that silence of daily life; giving one's life little by little.

319

Once capital becomes an idol and guides people's decisions,
once greed for money presides over the entire socioeconomic system,
it ruins society, it condemns and enslaves men and women, it destroys human
fraternity, it sets people against one another and, as we clearly see,
it even puts at risk our common home, sister and mother earth.

320

The wedding at Cana is repeated in every generation, in every family, in every one of us and our efforts to let our hearts find rest in strong love, fruitful love and joyful love.

321

The joys and sorrows of each are felt by all. That is what it means to be a family!

322

That is Christian hope: the future is in God's hands!
History makes sense because it dwells in God's goodness.

323

The depletion of conjugal love spreads resentment in relationships. And often this disintegration "collapses" onto the children.

324

The crowd is struck by the miracle
of the multiplication of the loaves;
but the gift Jesus offers is the *fullness of life*
for a hungering mankind.

325

Thus celebration is not lazily lounging
in an armchair, or the euphoria of foolish
escape. No, celebration is first and foremost
a loving and grateful look at work well done;
we celebrate work.

326

No cell is so isolated that it is shut
to the Lord, none.

327

When a corrupt person's private situation becomes complicated,
he knows all the loopholes to escape,
as did the dishonest steward of the Gospel.

328

Do not forget: the Lord comes, and if you feel a longing to improve, to be better, it is the Lord knocking at your door.

329

May the power of Christ, which brings freedom and service, be felt in so many hearts afflicted by war, persecution and slavery.

330

There is the language of the mind, thinking; the language of the heart, loving; the language of hands, making. And these three languages all join together to create the harmony of the person.

331

A society without mothers would be a dehumanized society, for mothers are always, even in the worst moments, witnesses of tenderness, dedication and moral strength.

332

People who perform in the circus create beauty, they are creators of beauty. And this is good for the soul. How much we need beauty!

333

It is precisely the oblivion of God, and not his glorification, which generates violence.

334

The globalization of hope, a hope which springs up from peoples and takes root among the poor, must replace the globalization of exclusion and indifference!

335

For the Church, the option for the poor is primarily a theological category rather than a cultural, sociological, political or philosophical one.

Nguyen Phuong Trang
Vietnam

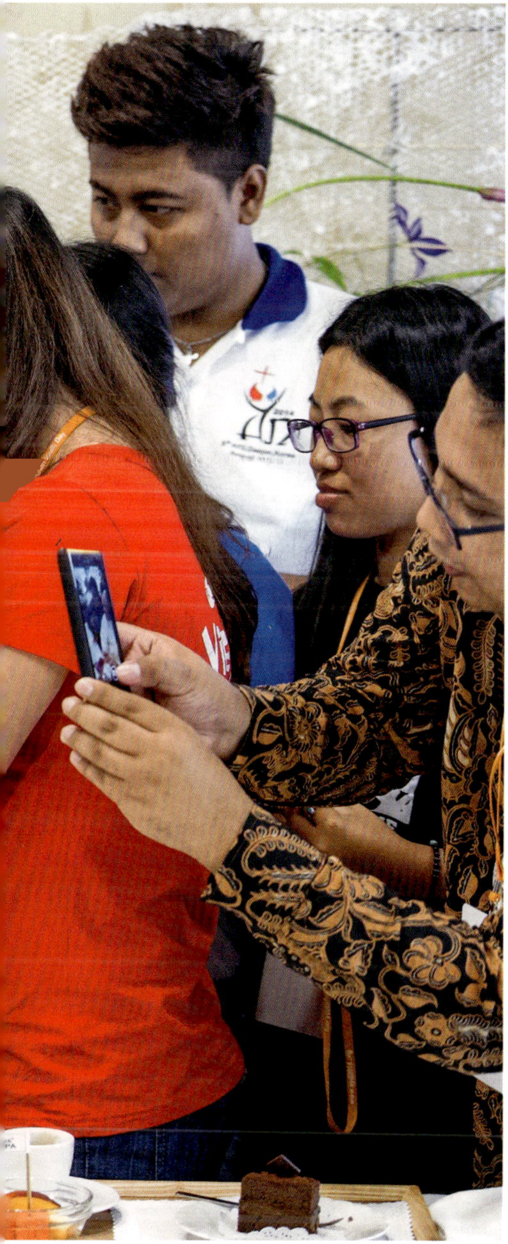

336

Youth is a time of high ideals. I often say that it is really sad to see a young person who is out of work.

337

It is sad to find "watered-down" Christians, who seem like watered-down wine. One cannot tell whether they are Christian or worldly, like watered-down wine; one cannot tell whether it is wine or water!

338

In Him it is possible to find interior peace and the strength to face different life situations every day, even the heaviest and most difficult. No one has ever heard of a sad saint with a mournful face.

339

Divisions among Christians, while they wound the Church, wound Christ; and divided, we cause a wound to Christ: the Church is indeed the body of which Christ is the Head.

340

The important thing is not to give in to the temptation of conflict, but to reject all violence. It is possible to dialogue, to listen, to plan together, and in this manner to overcome suspicion and prejudice and to build an ever more secure, peaceful and inclusive co-existence.

341

The salvific work of Christ is not exhausted with his Person and in the span of his earthly life; it continues through the Church, the sacrament of God's love and tenderness for mankind.

342

This beautiful and genuine predisposition is necessary to meet, understand, dialogue with, appreciate and relate to brothers in a respectful and sincere way – without this predisposition it is not possible to offer truly joyous and credible service and testimony.

343

The Gospel is the word of life: it does not oppress people, on the contrary, it frees those who are slaves to the many evil spirits of this world: the spirit of vanity, attachment to money, pride, sensuality....

344

The difference between man and woman is not meant to stand in opposition, or to subordinate, but is for the sake of communion and generation, always in the image and likeness of God.

345

We are called to live not as one without the others, above or against the others, but one with the others, for the others, and in the others. This means to accept and witness in harmony the beauty of the Gospel.

346

May our concrete solidarity not diminish especially with regard to the families who are experiencing more difficult situations due to illness, unemployment, discrimination, the need to emigrate....

347

Our needs, even if legitimate, are not as urgent as those
of the poor, who lack the basic necessities of life.
We often speak of the poor.

348

Each individual Christian and every community is called
to be an instrument of God for the liberation and promotion
of the poor, and for enabling them to be fully a part of society.
This demands that we be docile and attentive to the cry
of the poor and to come to their aid.

349

Each one must do his part in taking on the attitude of the Good Shepherd, who knows each one of his sheep and excludes no one from his infinitive love!

350

The disciples reason in "marketing" terms, but Jesus substitutes the logic of *buying* with another logic, the logic of *giving*.

351

It is grievous but there are divisions, there are many divided Christians, we have split amongst ourselves. But we all have something in common: we all believe in Jesus Christ, the Lord. We all believe in the Father, in the Son, and in the Holy Spirit, and we all walk together, we are on the journey. Let us help one another!

352

A good father *knows how to wait and knows how to forgive* from the depths of his heart. Certainly, he also knows how to correct with firmness: he is not a weak father, submissive and sentimental.

353

Let us pray that, with the help of the Lord and the cooperation of all men and women of good will, there will spread ever further a culture of encounter, capable of bringing down all the walls which still divide the world, and that no longer will innocent people be persecuted and even killed on account of their belief and their religion. Where there is a wall, there is a closed heart. We need bridges, not walls!

354

In order to resolve the problems in their relationships, men and women need to speak to one another more, listen to each other more, get to know one another better, love one another more.

355

Some think that sanctity is to close your eyes and to look like a holy icon. No! This is not sanctity! Sanctity is something greater, deeper, which God gives us. Indeed, it is precisely in living with love and offering one own Christian witness in everyday affairs that we are called to become saints.

356

If we are not able to forgive ourselves, then we are no longer able to forgive period.
A house in which the words "I'm sorry" are never uttered begins to lack air,
and the flood waters begin to choke those who live inside.

357

In our day, the problem no longer seems to be the invasive presence of the father so much as his absence, his inaction. Fathers are sometimes so concentrated on themselves and on their work and at times on their career that they even forget about the family.

358

A people which forgets its own past, its history and its roots, has no future, it is a dull people. Memory, if it is firmly based on justice and rejects hatred and all desire for revenge, makes the past a source of inspiration for the building of a future of serene coexistence. It also makes us realize the tragedy and pointlessness of war.

359

In order to be "imitators of Christ" in the face of a poor or sick person, we must not be afraid to look him in the eye and to draw near with tenderness and compassion, and to touch him and embrace him.

360

Prayer is the very root of peace. Peace is always possible and our prayer is at the root of peace. Prayer disseminates peace.

361

Thanks to Baptism we were introduced into communion with God and we are no longer at the mercy of evil and sin, but [rather] we receive the love, the tenderness, the mercy of the heavenly Father.

362

The Church is not a static reality, inert, an end in herself, but is on a continual journey through history, towards that ultimate and marvelous end that is the Kingdom of Heaven.

363

Jesus did not come into the world to be in a parade, but to be seen! He did not come for this. Jesus is the path and *a path is for walking and following*.

364

Jesus has come to bring joy to
all people for all time.

365

There is a close link between the hope of a people and the harmony among generations. The joy of children causes the parents' hearts to beat and reopens the future. Children are the joy of the family and of society. They are not a question of reproductive biology, nor one of the many ways to fulfil oneself, much less a possession of their parents....

GIUSEPPE COSTA (1946: GELA, ITALY)
A Salesian priest and journalist, Giuseppe Costa began his work in schools and with youth animation. He specialized in Pastoral Theology at the Pontifical Salesian University in Rome and completed a master's in Journalism at Marquette University (Wisconsin, USA). Costa, a visiting lecturer in Journalism and Publishing at the Pontifical Salesian University, taught at the University of Catania and the Luiss in Rome. Since 2007, he has been in charge of the Vatican Publishing House and was nominated Counselor of the Pontifical Council for Social Communications. His numerous publications include: *Parole attorno ai media* (Sciascia, 2002), *Dentro la fotografia* (Edizioni della Meridiana, 2002), *Dietro il giornale* (Las, 2004), *Editoria, media e religione* (Lev, 2009). He collaborated with Franco Zangrilli and published *Giornalismo e Letteratura* (Sciascia, 2005); with Angelo Paoluzi he cowrote *Giornalismo. Teoria e pratica* (Las, 2006), and *Giornalismo e Religione* (Lev, 2012), *Jorge Mario Bergoglio – Pope Francis, Thoughts and Words for the Soul* (White Star Publishers, 2014).

PHOTO CREDITS

COVER: © Vatican Media
BACK COVER: *left*: ©L'Osservatore Romano; *center*: Rossella Apostoli/123RF; *right*: ©L'Osservatore Romano

pages 2-3, ©L'Osservatore Romano
1, Exploderl/iStockphoto
2 and 3, ©L'Osservatore Romano
4, Worradirek Muksab/123RF
5 and 6, valbar/iStockphoto
7 and 8, Svetlana Alyuk/123RF
9 and 10, 2630ben/iStockphoto
11 and 12, ©L'Osservatore Romano
13 and 14, ©L'Osservatore Romano
15 and 16, Monika Gniot/123RF
17 and 18, Anett Bakos/123RF
19, freeartist/123RF
20 and 21, Malgorzata Kistryn/123RF
22, Iryna Bort/123RF
23 and 24, Christopher Badzioch/iStockphoto
25 and 26, ©L'Osservatore Romano
27 and 28, ©L'Osservatore Romano
29 and 30, Angelo Lano/123RF
31 and 32, stevecoleimages/iStockphoto
33 and 34, Denis Tabler/123RF
35, Vladimir Seliverstov/123RF, Vladimir Seliverstov/123RF
36 and 37, Irina Schmidt/123RF
38 and 39, Irina Tischenko/123RF
40, stevanzz/123RF
41 and 42, kotenko/123RF
43 and 44, cinoby/iStockphoto
45 and 46, ©L'Osservatore Romano
47 and 48, Anek Suwannaphoom/123RF
49 and 50, Sun Time/iStockphoto
51 and 52, FamVeld/iStockphoto
53 and 54, Sergey Galushko/123RF
55 and 56, Yanika Panfilova/123RF
57 and 58, fullempty/123RF, Andrey Prokuronov/123RF
59 and 60, Kevin Miller/iStockphoto
61 and 62, Shuchun Ke/123RF
63 and 64, Elena Ray/123RF
65 and 66, ©L'Osservatore Romano
67 and 68, Pavel Timofeev/123RF
69 and 70, kho/123RF
71 and 72, SANCHAI LOONGROONG/123RF
73 and 74, Linda Vostrovska/123RF
75 and 76, ©L'Osservatore Romano
77 and 78, ©L'Osservatore Romano
79, andreanita/123RF
80 and 81, Roksana Bashyrova/123RF
82 and 83, kelifamily/123RF
84 and 85, picsfive/123RF, Ivan Mikhaylov/123RF
86 and 87, ©L'Osservatore Romano
88 and 89, ©L'Osservatore Romano
90 and 91, Naphat Chantaravisoot/123RF
92 and 93, mrfish09/123RF
94 and 95, ©L'Osservatore Romano
96 and 97, ©L'Osservatore Romano
98 and 99, Anton Petrus/123RF
100 and 101, RawFile/iStockphoto
102 and 103, blueone/123RF, PRASIT KRAISUNGNOEN/123RF
104 and 105, Qi Feng/123RF
106 and 107, Dean Fikar/123RF
108, Alexander Raths/123RF, Miroslawa Drozdowski/123RF
109, Olha Rohulya/123RF
110 and 111, Alexey Stiop/123RF
112 and 113, Ivaylo Sarayski/123RF
114, Naphat Chantaravisoot/123RF, Chrstiankeller/iStockphoto
115 and 116, udra/123RF
117 and 118, ©L'Osservatore Romano
119 and 120, ©L'Osservatore Romano
121 and 122, ©L'Osservatore Romano
123, Matthew Gibson/123RF
124 and 125, Thittaya Janyamethakul/123RF
126 and 127, Richard Semik/123RF
128 and 129, Vladimir Salman/123RF
130 and 131, Oleg Tovkach/123RF
132 Noam Armonn/123RF
133 and 134, tonarinokeroro/123RF
135 and 136, valio84sl/iStockphoto
137 and 138, Pratya Chutipattarasakul/123RF
139, jasiek03/123RF
140 and 141, Rossella Apostoli/123RF
142 and 143, ©L'Osservatore Romano
144 and 145, ©L'Osservatore Romano
146, suriko8/123RF, Vaclav Volrab/123RF

147 and 148, Naphat Chantaravisoot/123RF, CHIRASAK TOLERTMONGKOL/123RF
149, Carolina K. Smith, M.D./123RF, designpics/123RF
150 and 151, PeopleImages/iStockphoto
152, Aleksandr Makarenko/123RF, Andrew Howe/iStockphoto
153 and 154, Alexia Khruscheva/123RF
155 and 156, Erkki Alvenmod/123RF
157 and 158, ©L'Osservatore Romano
159 and 160, ©L'Osservatore Romano
161 and 162, Mykola Ivashchenko/123RF, Dmitry Maslov/123RF
163 and 164, bogumil/123RF
165, Worradirek Muksab/123RF
166 and 167, Mazuryk Mykola/123RF
168, hansslegers/iStockphoto, hansslegers/iStockphoto
169 and 170, Olha Rohulya/123RF
171, andreiuc88/123RFLynn Bystrom/123RF
172, photographereddie/iStockphoto, FamVeld/iStockphoto
173 and 174, Alexander Raths/123RF, Konstantin Yolshin/123RF
175 and 176, Betty Shelton/123RF
177 and 178, fotoguy22/iStockphoto, Mark Kostich/iStockphoto
179 and 180, ©L'Osservatore Romano
181 and 182, ©L'Osservatore Romano
183 and 184, DenisTangneyJr/iStockphoto
185 and 186, ramblingman/123RF
187 and 188, Steve Byland/123RF, humpata/123RF
189 and 190, Ant Clausen/123RF
191 and 192, leekris/123RF
193 and 194, Alex Smith/iStockphoto
195 and 196, Artem Povarov/123RF
197 and 198, ©L'Osservatore Romano
199 and 200, ©L'Osservatore Romano
201 and 202, Bas Meelker/123RF
203 and 204, byrdyak/123RF, Vladimir Salman/123RF
205 and 206, Olha Rohulya/123RF
207 and 208, Olha Rohulya/123RF
209 and 210, lakhesis/123RF
211, Mathew Hayward/123RF
212 and 213, pat138241/123RF, Visarute Angkatavanich/123RF
214 and 215, Ivan Andrienko/123RF
216, gorillaimages/123RF
217 and 218, ©L'Osservatore Romano
219 and 220, ©L'Osservatore Romano
221 and 222, Janis Smits/123RF
223 and 224, Anton Petrus/123RF, Dmytro Vietrov/123RF
225 and 226, Maria Elena Pueyo Ruiz/123RF
227 and 228, Eric Gevaert/123RF
229 and 230, Michael Pettigrew/123RF
231, Michael Pettigrew/123RF
232 and 233, ©L'Osservatore Romano
234 and 235, ©L'Osservatore Romano
236 and 237, Riccardo Farina/123RF
238 and 239, Anek Suwannaphoom/123RF
240 and 241, filonmar/iStockphoto
242 and 243, Oliver Taylor/123RF
244, PaylessImages/123RF, PaylessImages/123RF
245 and 246, Photolyric/iStockphoto
247 and 248, Ievgenii Biletskyi/123RF, PaylessImages/123RF
249 and 250, fotoVoyager/iStockphoto
251 and 252, Dmitry Pichugin/123RF, Galyna Andrushko/123RF
253 and 254, Photolyric/iStockphoto
255, Vladimir Voronin/123RF
256 and 257, ©L'Osservatore Romano
258 and 259, ©L'Osservatore Romano
260 and 261, tomas1111/123RF
262 and 263, aloha 17/iStockphoto
264, Liima10/iStockphoto
265 and 266, andreiuc88/123RF
267 and 268, Debbie Orlean/123RF
269 and 270, Mark Bridger/123RF
271 and 272, Olha Rohulya/123RF
273 and 274, Steve Byland/123RF
275, Steve Byland/123RF
276 and 277, ©L'Osservatore Romano
278 and 279, ©L'Osservatore Romano
280 and 281, ©L'Osservatore Romano
282 and 283, subbotina/123RF
284 and 285, annems/123RF
286 and 287, Irina Schmidt/123RF
288 and 289, dra schwartz/iStockphoto
290 and 291, Dmitry Travnikov/123RF
292 and 293, Steve Byland/123RF
294, snehit/123RF
295 and 296, Volodymyr Goinyk/123RF, Igor Goncharenko/123RF
297 and 298, Aleksandr Makarenko/123RF
299 and 300, Roksana Bashyrova/123RF, Mikel Martinez De Osaba/123RF
301 and 302, ©L'Osservatore Romano
303, ©L'Osservatore Romano
304, ©L'Osservatore Romano
305 and 306, ©L'Osservatore Romano
307 and 308, danymages/123RF
309 and 310, Alexey Stiop/123RF
311, Alexey Stiop/123RF
312 and 313, Nikola Nikolovski/123RF, Vaclav Volrab/123RF
314 and 315, Igor Yaruta/123RF
316 and 317, Jacek Nowak/123RF
318, Konrad Kerker/123RF
319, Vichaya Kiatying-Angsulee/123RF, Igor Goncharenko/123RF
320 and 321, dotshock/123RF
322 and 323, ©L'Osservatore Romano
324 and 325, ©L'Osservatore Romano
326 and 327, Aslinah Safar/123RF, Luka Vunduk/123RF
328 and 329, Olha Rohulya/123RF
330 and 331, belchonock/123RF
332 and 333, Casanowe/iStockphoto
334 and 335, ©L'Osservatore Romano
336 and 337, ©L'Osservatore Romano
338 and 339, ©L'Osservatore Romano
340 and 341, Chaiyagorn Phermphoon/123RF
342, Zdenek Rosenthaler/123RF, Sonya Etchison/123RF
343 and 344, Jacek Nowak/123RF
345 and 346, Berangere Duforets/123RF, Berangere Duforets/123RF
347 and 348, ©L'Osservatore Romano
349 and 350, ©L'Osservatore Romano
351 and 352, Olha Rohulya/123RF
353 and 354, Olena Suvorova/123RF
355, sergeyp/123RF
356 and 357, Dean Fikar/iStockphoto
358 and 359, Leonid Tit/123RF
360 and 361, ©L'Osservatore Romano
362 and 363, ©L'Osservatore Romano
364 and 365, ©L'Osservatore Romano

The quotations in this volume were drawn from Holy Masses, Pastoral Visits, Meetings, Interviews, General Audiences, the Angelus and Regina Coeli, the encyclical Laudato Sì, the Apostolic Exhortation Evangelii Gaudium, and Twitter.

Text and selected quotes edited by
Giuseppe Costa

Texts of the Holy Father courtesy of the
Libreria Editrice Vaticana

Project editor
Valeria Manferto De Fabianis

Editorial assistant
Laura Accomazzo

Graphic layout
Maria Cucchi

Piazzale Luigi Cadorna, 6
20123 Milan, Italy
www.whitestar.it

Translation: Irina Oryschevic

ISBN 978-88-544-2176-9
1 2 3 4 5 6 29 28 27 26 25

Printed in Türkiye